GW01287611

ICE BOUND

Nicky Mesch

KFS

NEWTON-LE-WILLOWS

Published in the United Kingdom in 2016
by The Knives Forks And Spoons Press,
122 Birley Street,
Newton-le-Willows,
Merseyside,
WA12 9UN.

ISBN 978-1-909443-72-3

Acknowledgements:

'hooked' and a version of 'the words' appeared in issue 58 of *Tears in the Fence.*

Thanks to: David Caddy for his wonderfully encouraging 'rejection' letters; Alec Newman for taking a chance on a fairy-tale unknown; Kate Kirk for her expertise in marketing the local launch; Katherine Gallagher and Jackie Wills for workshops that facilitated two of the poems in this narrative; Linda Rose Parkes and Colin Scott, who offered invaluable feedback, not only on many of the individual poems, but also on the first draft of the manuscript; Christine Journeaux, Heike Oberg and Sharon Champion for their thoughtful insights and unwavering support for 'the ice story;' the members of the former writers circle for their feedback on the early poems; and finally, to my family for their belief in me.

Cover image:

Paul VanDerWerf

LOTTERY FUNDED

Supported using public funding by
ARTS COUNCIL
ENGLAND

contents

prologue

I. the gleaming dark

II. a chill wind

III. words unspoken

IV. blood-light

V. sending a message

VI. a bold proposal

VII. vows

epilogue

prologue

second best

they say your fourth wife
has given you a daughter –

a half-sister
I'll never meet

odd-looking thing
will you hold her

slipped easy into the world
will you raise her at the castle

at least this time the mother survived
will you watch her dance

no frost on this one
give her a name

I

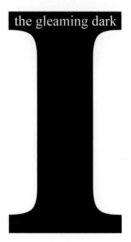

the gleaming dark

come to me

in darkness
bristling with fur

silky-pawed
silver-eyed wolf
tracking tender prey
through shadow's heart

come to me
so silent swift
air barely trembles
when you pounce

devour me

hooked

why doesn't that girl
tie a leash around your neck
and be done with it?

his Ma never gets it right –

not a leash
but a line hooked
both ends

spooling silver thin
across the water

fragile at first

any pull
would barely sting

but each time
he's with her

he could stumble
the final kiss

hook the next
cold clumsy
to her breast

painstakingly
playing it out

as he's rowed
back to shore

he'll secure his end
barb-deep

the glint of it

one strand thicker

harder to cut

Birch

if hell is fire
is heaven ice?

* * *

I didn't think
it would be like this

even frost-burnt
and bitten

Tom comes back

propping the door
while he tells me
about the horses –

Dancer's off her food
the foal's coming along

or he'll sprawl
in a chair by the fire

to watch
while I ready
for bed

can't touch yet
but I can look

he can make a look
last hours

* * *

so much a part of me
I'd   forgotten
      almost

but last night
silver light picked out
the scars on my back

the chair scraped
he leant close –

                                        who?

...Birch

                                        which one?

the first

                                        did she last?

...   ...   *...no*

                                        good

* * *

I needn't have feared
he'd ask more

he trusts I did
as he'd have done

given a swift clean death –

if only I had

* * *

too bold
if I looked her
dead in the eye

sly
if I averted my gaze

impudent
for asking questions

sullen
if I asked none

feather-head
if I laughed
or skipped
or sang
evil
any song
evil
that wasn't a hymn to her

evil
god

* * *

she left her lifework –

saving souls
among the nomads
of the shifting sands –

to risk the ice
to save me

* * *

first lesson

she had the maidservants
shroud the windows

and I might have sat
far from candlelight
to dull my haze

but for the yearning
of my gloved fingers

to chase spiky black markings
across page after page after
water-crinkled page

* * *

second lesson

she stripped
my chambers of books

had them piled
in the courtyard

over-loved
they refused to burn –

she ordered me help
carry them to the ferry

to smoulder
in the village

* * *

third lesson

she thrust
her worn scripture
into my un-gloved hand

its spine brittle-
                    broke
  in the fall

before I could expl ...

d
e
r
a
o
her cane s

* * *

some days she'd start slow

tread the darkening room
in measured steps

others she'd almost
trip
to keep pace

with the rapture
spilling
her cracked lips

bustling
heavy
circles
until
she spun
to stop

eyes tight blue
scaly hands skyward

crow body
            quivering
over me

calling to
a father
            who
no matter

how many hours
  my knees
            cried
repentance

would never
grant mercy

to a creature
such as me

* * *

why pray if I'll never be forgiven?

h	r	r	t
e	e	i	h
r	d	b	e
	|	b	
c		o	a
a		n	i
n		n	r
e		e	
		d	

* * *

it would have been so easy
to catch her hand
at lesson

or creep
into her bedchamber
while she slept

* * *

I couldn't bring myself to touch her

* * *

the servants at the castle

the girl whose fall I broke
without thinking

the cook I backed into

the pink-nose kitten
that leapt on me

~~the child –~~

whether I list
two
twenty-score
more –

unintended
every one

but if I touched Birch…

* * *

mortal afraid
I'd snap
lash back –

the creature
they believed me to be

* * *

cook stopped over-
salting my food

the maidservants forgot
to leave pins in my dresses
or grit in my boots

two books even slid
under my pillow

't ain't right, mistress
and you the crippled king's daughter

yet
the corridors clattered empty
the minute lessons began

* * *

even a creature
with blood
on her hands

can beg forgiveness –

I held out a hand

look, no blood

* * *

the longer the cane

the more
        enduring
                the lesson

* * *

did you know what she was
when you sent her to me?

* * *

she kept calling out

merciful father

the only father
I could think of
was you

* * *

her conviction –

if I wasn't
doing evil

I was
thinking evil

* * *

I was beyond hope

* * *

head down
palms pious

knees numb
beyond aching

frost taking on
the gloom

I'd wrap myself
in imagining

ice-needles
streaking
the length of her cane

splintering
her up-stretched arm

ice-veining
her neck

her mouth
frozen
O
blue eyes
frosting
disbelief

as forever after
I used her
perfectly
positioned
arm

as a cloak-hook

* * *

but if I started

how to trust
I'd stop?

* * *

touch anyone

cause one more living
creature to freeze

your arms will be bound
till you go to your grave

your edict still hangs
limp in the hallway

* * *

the servants taught me to count

by tallying the bodies I froze
the day I learnt to walk

they could never agree
if my mother was the first –

childbirth claims so many –

they say she refused
to give me up

but held me held me held
so tight
they had to
p r i s e   m e   away

they say she strayed
into delirium

called on darker spirits
to protect me –

and cold death
being so close

was the first to answer

* * *

every governess
that came after Birch
was made to bear her name –

one of your edicts
I thought

but it was the servants' doing –

whether for them or me
certain protection from you

* * *

she's not buried
in the churchyard

I wonder where they put her

* * *

if she hadn't refused to rotate classrooms
                given my ice a chance to build
if I'd muted my defiance
if she'd swapped thin soles for snow-ridge boots
if my frost-haze hadn't inflamed her

if she hadn't left the nomads
if you'd sniffed the zealot in her
if I hadn't been beyond salvation
touched her quick
if her god any god had existed
answered either of our cries
if her cane had been less eager
if she hadn't slipped mid-
stroke
if her spine had been less brittle
if piety hadn't worn me rigid wrong
if the servants hadn't scarpered

if I could stop
the
r e l e n t l e s s
c r a c k l e
o f m y i c e

g l e a m i n g

t o w a r d h e r

i n t h e d a r k

* * *

merciful father

it burns

a man of your word?

I was taught
that a man's honour lies
on the strength of his word
                                        and yet

the night I came into this world
swiftly ushered my mother out of it –
            they say you threatened to kill me

the day I learnt to walk
perished half the castle –
            you threatened to kill me

the day you exiled me
to the lodge on the lake –
            you threatened to kill me

the time I returned
for my marriage-making ball
and not one nobleman
would dance with me –
            you threatened to kill me

after I stole away
with your best stable-boy
and three favourite horses –
            you wrote threatening to kill me

the first time
I dared ask permission
to govern my mother's lands –

each time I write thereafter –

            you respond with a promise to kill me

which begs a question

a certain truth

think that girl'd still have you in her bed
if any of her kind could stand her touch?

sometimes it's easier to rise
to bait

king's daughter, Ma
she'd have us both

for bitter silence

grievance day

heard from the old baron lately?

not yet

everyone's asking

I know

the chicken thief
the tavern gang
the ruckus at south farm
they're stacking up

Tom, I know
I'll write again to remind him

can't you take it?
did last time

careful

let your decisions stand, didn't he?

he had to –
couldn't admit to dozing off

but if he's starting to lose it

he's still the best of a bad lot, Tom
my father will never give me the reins
not even for grievance day

if he hears the old baron's past it
he'll send someone far worse

we can't go through that again

wouldn't be like last time
the villagers look to you –

lifeblood
the elders call it

what your melted ice
does to the land

it's still my father's proxy
who decides the crops we grow

not lately

which is why
we need to tread soft

but you're right, Tom
grievance day can't wait

I'll write another letter
to the old baron

if one of your lads
can deliver it

* * *

lifeblood

* * *

if ~~only~~ that were true

II

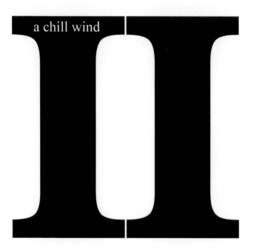

a chill wind

…ice demons

keep to the snow plains of the north
spend their summers hunting walrus and wrestling polar bears
their winters storming the women of the south…

an ice demon looks for heat in a woman

the hotter the blood the better…

unending refrain

that I'll fall asleep
before I can cold-shoulder
Tom out of my bed

wake to an ice-
casket beside me

* * *

that one day
the blizzard in his head
will howl so it drowns
all thought of me

pull him north

* * *

that my father
will make good

on even one
of his promises –

send his army

appoint a steward
with a choke-grip

or succeed in finding me
a husband I can't refuse

* * *

might as well worry

about the border lords
stopping their squabbling
long enough to invade

or the mountain clans
looking to steal
more than sheep

or the nomads
of the shifting sands
raiding our horses

is that meant to
make me feel better?

a black ribbon day

the first I knew of the old baron's death –

your presence will not be required at the funeral

the rest of his successor's five page missive
listed the requirements for his inaugural visit

* * *

a season's respite
before he arrives

if only it were winter

used to be

nights he couldn't
lie beside me
he'd settle
in the chair watching
fire smoulder

but
lately he's taken
to standing at the frost-
cracked window

forever staring
north

un-
settling

do we need so many stable-lads, Tom?
those two don't even know how to ride

the horses like 'em
and they're demon with an axe

and they are demon
spawn

as Tom is

but not
ice
as Tom is

and as Cobb
Fin
Cully
and so many of the others
who dally a winter or two
before drifting north are

nor **fire**
as Ash the smithy's lad is
whose amber eyes slow-
burn the village girls

no, these latest two
are something darker

from the forest
watching quiet

a frosty reception

the old baron's widow
turned up yesterday
with her two daughters

three golden carriages
bristling with jewels

she offered me
her late husband's papers
for *three beds and some broth*

warned me not
to be too trusting
conciliatory
outspoken
obliging
or objectionable
when the new baron arrives

her daughters are beautiful
but bruised

the new baron refused
to take the older girl
in marriage

would have taken
the younger girl
without

so they fled

*   *   *

they'd expected to find me at the palace
had intended staying there
in keeping with our station

what happened to
three beds and some broth?
said Tom

because of my *infernal ice*
and my *loose country ways*
they chafe at staying at the lodge

when are they leaving?
said Tom

they could have sought refuge
with the village pastor
have we fallen so low?

or at one of the teaching houses
my girls need husbands high-born
not a wittering of frost-bitten women

or even at the old manor
with the clearest view of the mist
on the river mountains
a cobweb-festooned ruin
stinking of mould

Tom frayed quick
if they wanted fine things
should've stayed put

started to fray at me
why do you let 'em talk
to you that way

*   *   *

because everyone does

always has

except for him

he can't forget

the way they met
the night of the ball

tracking her frost-trail
from the balcony steps

to the cherry trees
by the castle's outer wall

the way she'd shimmer-
chimed in the silver light

the way she had looked at him

the way he'd knelt at her feet
to slice the frozen butterflies
from the skirts of her gown

the way his shiny-sharp knife
glinted as it cut

* * *

the way he'd refused
to let her dismiss him –

not till the butterflies dance, mistress

so she'd made him run
for her furs instead

his surprise
when his numb-clumsy feet
refused to fly

even then
determined
to push through
alive
with the pain

till he could duck and dive
the stable yard clatter

skidding in horse-shit
he should've been shovelling

oi Tom, get yer lazy ars-

dodging into shadow

catching his hand
on the door
of her carriage

to grab a slippery
mass of silky fur
already
desperate-wild
to get back

finding her
where he'd left her

the master's only daughter
humming soft

dancing alone
in the moonlight

* * *

the way she'd paused
to study him hard

as he fought to contain
the lush ripple
spilling
his arms

her breezy –

wrap them around you, Tom
warm them up for me

the smallest roughest lad
reeking of sweat
shit and piss –

and she wanted him to –

please, Tom

her almost-smile

I can't abide cold things
against my skin

picking up her skirts
as if to leave

so he'd wrapped himself
in tickling softness

that smelt of a girl
                    spun
from star-light and ice

who danced silver
circles on the grass

a dream he could never
have imagined –

yet the splinter
throbbing his hand
was real

* * *

he was used to curses
a clip on the ear –

she wouldn't stop
with her questions

prodding his answers –

as if she really wanted to know
about his Ma
three hulking brothers
life at the stables

do you get to choose which horses to ride, Tom?
do you wish you did?

his words tumbling over thoughts spilling into more words
till he was offering everything –

the constant pull to go north
the dreams that had started to fill his nights –
snow drift and howling ice

I live with a blizzard
in my head, mistress
drives me fierce mad at times

* * *

can't promise blizzard, Tom
but I can guarantee ice
stables too, though they're not up to much
the stable-master prefers ale to horses
so most of the work would fall to you

she couldn't be offering –

don't make me want
he wanted to say

and still she was slow dancing
talking quick –

about the nomads of the shifting sands
who called her star-fall –
daughter of the night sky

who gifted her a black stallion
their best horsemen couldn't break

full moon he swims across
stamps his hooves
till I open my window
I have to lock myself in, Tom
so I won't run out
and leap on his back
to plunge the lake
my fingers gripping his tangled mane
as I lean into him
urging faster faster faster
flying into the dark

her way of giving a smile
that wasn't a smile –

if I did any of that
I'd kill him

her hesitant –

you could though, Tom
if you came back with me

* * *

his gruff –

I'd kill to go with you

unsayable true –

Ma will kill me if I do

but your blisters

forget 'em

Tom we can't not yet
so you can stop that

right now

a surfeit of stable-lads

I can understand
the off-shoots
of an ice demon

being drawn
to this cold-cursed land

choosing to settle
for a spell

but demon seed
of fire and forest

and whatever
that new lad Bray is

why would they come?

why do they stay?

and why does Tom let them?

III

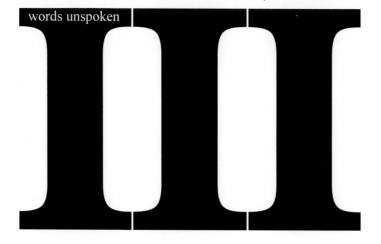

words unspoken

a matter of trust

the invitation
to the old baron's widow
and her daughters
came just in time

almost
I warned her
have a care –

unspoiled beauties
even those gentle-born
can lose their bloom
at the castle

tread clever
or your girls will likely end
passed from king
to nobleman
to gutter

but
if you let them
be found wanting –
and
if the crippled king's temper
runs true –

they might end here instead

forever exiled
in my service

at a teaching
or merchant house

any remaining bloom
frozen clean

* * *

but I couldn't
                    say such things

to a tattle-mouth
                    such as her

she wouldn't have listened anyway
Tom said

was it wrong of me
not to try?

names

that thing

as in

get that thing *from my sight*

daughter

as in

you are no daughter *of mine*

beloved

as in

what man would call you beloved

creature

as in

right cold wicked little

that girl

as in

that girl *doesn't love you*
that girl *will be the death of you*
that g-

ENOUGH, Ma
I'd be gone
but for that girl

cold-cursed

as in

come here, woman
put your cold-cursed *hands on me*

mistress

        as in

                mine

the words

I hadn't known
they could simmer
                    unseen

erupt at a slow grin

            h a n g   e x p o s e d

in the frost-light

            so fragile
I almost
snatched them back

his stillness
stopped me

I'd heard
such words

take root
in the heart –

I find them
in his eyes

his rough hands

even pulsing
under his skin –

already the urge
to use them again

but I resist

wanting him to use them
in return

my love my love my love my love my love my love my love my love my love
my love my love my love my love my love my love my love my love my love
my love my love my love my love my love my love my love my love my love
my love my love my love my love my love my love my love my love my love
my love my love my love my love my love my love my love my love my love
my love my love my love my love my love my love love me my love my love
my love my love my love my love my love my love my love my love my love
my love my love my love my love my love my love my love my love my love
my love my love my love my love my love my love my love my love my love
my love my love my love my love my love my love my love my love my love
love me my love my love my love my love my love my love my love my love
my love my love my love my love Tom my love my love my love my love
my love my love my love my love my love my love my love my love love me
my love my love my love my love my love my love my love my love my love
my love my love my love my love my love my love my love my love my love
my love my love my love my love my love my love my love my love my love
my love my love my love my love my love my love my love my love my love
my love my love love me my love my love my love my love my love my love
my love my love my love my love my love my love my love my love my love
my love my love my love my love my love my love my love my love my love
my love my love my love my love my love my love my love my love my love
my love my love my love my love my love my love my love my love my love
my love my love my love my love my love my love my love my love my love

a strange thing

I don't know how I let it happen

but the hand that helped me down
from the carriage wasn't Tom's

skin to ungloved skin
dropped quick

Cobb's fingers
already blackening

Tom reached for his axe

called to Ash for heat
seal the wound

Cobb chattering
                    white
don't understand

cold-dazed
                  blue
thought I could touch
same as

                                        swift
                              done
only three fingers
                              lost

worth it
to have touched you
mistress

offspring
of ice demon

as is Tom

yet
only Tom

can suffer my touch

compromise

the old baron's younger girl
waited
till the horses were hitched
the carriages loaded

before she asked
to speak to me
alone

I want to stay

that's not-

and marry Ash

but-

he's from fire
a smithy's lad
I know

your mothe-

it's your permission
we need

that's not quite-

I have to marry
and quick

if Ash-

not Ash

oh?

I can't

please don't make me say

I see

but surely your mothe-

calls me liar –

so-

she'll see the truth
soon enough
everyone will

but if it's not-

Ash says he'll have me anyway

I still don't-

I thought you'd understand

I do but-

the old smithy's fading

I know but-

Ash has ideas and skill
I have jewels and coin

that's not-

it'll work
it has to work

but-

and this way
I get to choose

you of all people
can understand that

can't you?

* * *

if you help us
mama won't take this light –

by the time she's through
you and your-
you'll be the talk
of the cornered lands

I thought we already were

* * *

please, Mistress
I want this

and I know
he'll protect me

you don't need
to marry for that

but she does

until I can change it

* * *

if I can change it

blood-light

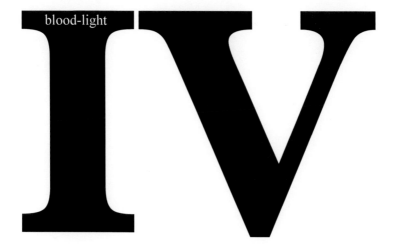

IV

close

come here, woman

just once I wish

what, love?

doesn't matter

what?

say it again

come here

not that

woman

Tom!

come here first

you want me
come and get me

* * *

I will not   will not   will not   wish for more

dance-card

what've you got there?

my dance-card from the ball

thought no one'd dance with you

they didn't
my father filled it in

look at the names, Tom

the western barons
the border lords
the guardian of the crystal towers

let me see that

I was such a fool

my marriage-making ball
that's what he called it

the hours I spent
on that butterfly gown

and all along

he meant you to get rid of 'em

no wonder
he said what he did
when I ran

love

but look at the rest, Tom –
all four princes of the blistering isles
the masters of glitter-stone and spice

he's looking across the water

I think so

one good thing –
if he's looking across the water
he won't be looking here

will he?

father –

no matter
how many kingdoms
you gather

they'll scatter when you die

men

the only ones
I saw in exile –

the crook-back gardener
who chased frost from the gardens

the ferryman who pushed off
if I skipped too close

the village pastor
who lectured me monthly
from the far end
of the long corridor

my uncle the king's brother
who visited
                    once
to see if
            I look like my mother –

that night at the castle

one hundred
princes and noblemen
bristled the ballroom

was it any wonder I ran?

demons unleashed

the sea demons would have killed me
if Tom hadn't arrived –

they were all
so slippery huge
brutish quick

a writhingrushingwhirlpool
that whipped
shore lake night
to frenzy

flung me about

before knocking me down
to snarl over me

the sound of my voice
had them drooling

each rip of my dress
made them yelp

skin bared
set them baying

I was weak

closed my eyes
to draw blizzard
so fierce

I could
            almost
feel ice-
shroud forming

a rough manacle
at my wrist

flung me against
a twisted tree

then the biggest
was upon me

fish-rot
crushing me

barnacles
scraping me

his eyes –
moonlight
on a dancing sea

I hated him
for their beauty

in a face
huge-mottled

more scar
than skin

tusk tooth bone
dug into me

as the salt wind raged
and his pack circled

quivering for blood

I let him shred me bare
I let him tear my gloves
I let him bristle-
brine all over me

I let him get so close

still my ice wouldn't hold

I had to hook my fingers
through his gills

lock limpet-tight
to stop him
wriggling free

croon cold promise
in his whelk-crusted ear

then I caught breath

pressed my mouth
to his barbed lips

held fast

till my frigid fire
consumed him

* * *

as their leader
shattered

the demon pack
scattered lakewards

salt crystals
glinting the night

clutching my gown
I got to my feet –

their signal
to surge back on me
in a seething roar

* * *

a sea siren's voice
is enchantment
impure –

I am no sea siren
have no wave-song

to lull a mariner
onto jagged rocks
                                        or calm
a sea demon frenzy

but I have a half-hum song
that had half-killed Tom
one fear-etched day

I used it now
to keep them at bay

them circling me
me circling back

                    crooning
as soothing

as my jumping
wits would allow

I never doubted Tom
was on his way
                                        but
hurry my love hurry

* * *

Tom stormed the shore
in a rush of stable-lads –

all feral fierce
swinging their axes
with lethal grace

blade
            clashed
on blade
            screamed
to bone

a blood-filled dance
in the howling night

Tom started to hack
a path to me

was submerged
in a writhe
of sea demons

I leapt on the closest –
a limpet again –

salt burn in my eyes
on my skin
in every breath

as the scaly monster
bellowed and whirled
trying to scrape free of me

he shattered quicker
than the first –

though
            painful
                  slow

*   *   *

I was still spitting salt
when Tom scooped me up

dumped me
among the roots
of a fallen tree

                              stay
but –
                              STAY

axe already in flight
where a sea demon sprang

Tom had killed before
                        for me –
a murky act

no murkiness now
but his true self –

half demon
pure warrior

unleashed

*   *   *

was I now
some puny thing

that trembled
in a burrow
at the crashing night

keep DOWN, WOMAN

I ducked –
a harpoon sliced

splintered bark
behind me

I cowered deep

gripping my arm
in scratchy darkness

till my blood
flowed sulky

* * *

does my cold-curse only work
when I don't want it to?

* * *

I wanted Tom and his lads safe
I wanted the sea demons gone
I wanted not to feel

snowdrop small
I wanted to see what was happening
I wanted to be back at the lodge
frost-lace keeping guard
for it to be one of the nights
I could have Tom gruff-
tender in my bed

* * *

I want
holds no power
I wish
that's the charm

a struggle
to resist
its insidious pull

for a wish cast in fear –

a sprig of frost-flowers pressed
to a newborn's breast

hailstones the size of boulders
to crush a sea demon's head

ice-needles deadly enough
to pierce a sea demon's eye –

even the wisp of a wish –

to be able
            just once
                        to be held till dawn –

can quick-curdle to a curse
under a blood moon

          *   *   *

snow flakes
thick and soft

a
     drift
            of
                 starlight

cooling the battle-storm

chilling the last
of the sea demons

who scattered
                            yelping
towards the lake

Tom and his lads hot on their tails

          *   *   *

tie 'em tight
till they bleed

take 'em to the lodge
the dead-rot too

lay Cully
in the boat

we'll see him home
when we're done

* * *

his lads follow
without question –

a warrior pack

* * *

he made me stay hidden
till the shore held
only snow-light –

snow-light
and poor freckled Cully
who'd flamed
whenever I spoke

* * *

not a word
as grain by grit-grain
he brushed the salt from me

not a word
as he uncovered
each of my wounds

ferocious he ripped
a strip of his shirt
to bind my arm

but you're hurt too –

seeping slash
across his chest

bite marks
not mine
on his right shoulder

jagged gash
on his hip –

not a word
as he wrapped me
in his torn shirt

blood and his scent
cloaking me

overpowering
the stench of the sea

I met his eyes

silver
            savage
true

didn't flinch
when his thumb found
the cuts on my lip

but I winced
at the gentleness
of his kiss –

shivered close

to make him
kiss me harder

make the sting
because of him

* * *

I don't want them
kept prisoner
I want them dead

I mean it, Tom
if you won't do it
I will

* * *

not yet

sea demons don't attack
without reason

why you?

why now?

first we get answers
then you can have your way

* * *

when did he start giving orders?

when did I start to obey?

V

sending a message

~~*great and illustrious ruler*~~

~~the one true master of the cornered lands~~
~~conqueror of~~

dear father

a pack of sea demons blew in from the east yesterday
~~they were going to use me to send you a message -~~
they asked me to convey their extreme displeasure –

they ~~demand~~ respectfully ask that you stop your mariners
plundering the fathomless seas for tooth and tusk
trails of ~~butchered carcasses~~ blubber and good meat
~~bloating~~ rotting in their wake

they ~~insist~~ would like your seafarers to stop tormenting
the siren sprites of the eddying rocks
~~leaving them crushed empty of wave-song~~

land-born men –
even those ruled by the ~~crip-~~ king of the cornered lands –
~~will learn~~ are advised to abide by the laws that flow
from the spirit of the sea

if your men don't, father, the pack vowed to return
~~to unleash a dark tide on this land of women~~
to send an even stronger message

I hope you forgive the liberty, father
but I answered on your behalf

for a siren song

and a shipwreck
casket of gold

Bray the new lad
betrayed us

should've known
the horses never trusted him

Tom caught him
setting a fire
in the stables –

distraction from
the sea demon attack

he must have
spent weeks

securing ropes
to reach the waves
from the cliff-top

laying guide-stones
through the forest
to the island

perhaps he didn't want to-

he made his choice

no dungeon at the lodge

we kept them chained
to the pillars
in the long corridor

I still hear their screams

two tortuous days
to get answers

kingdom small as yours
can't be weak

we couldn't spare Bray
couldn't risk any of them

get used to it

Tom put three to the blade
returned their bodies to the sea

I took care of the rest

vile slithery reeking

mesmerising monsters –

if they had approached
without weapons

asked me to intercede
on their behalf

would I have listened?

what he'll never forget

that night at her father's castle
the place she should have been safest
held most precious –

not one guard
not one servant
had come looking for her

* * *

misguided
such trust
in her invulnerability

* * *

what she can never know

as he knelt before her
slicing the frozen butterflies
from her skirts

blade catching silver

he kept thinking

if I cut you here
or here
or here
or here

you'd die

* * *

and she
oblivious
talk-talk-talking to him
punctuating every sentence
every thought with

...Tom *...Tom* *...Tom*

her hold tightening
her pull strengthening

claiming him
with every

...Tom

took my breath

you in that butterfly gown

where did that come from?

just sayin'

accursed daughter

yet again you fail to communicate
the crux of the matter –

how many sea demons?
what devastation did they wreak?
did they return to the waves or turn their tails inland?

how many times must you be reminded
you hold no authority to speak on my behalf

I can only hope you were not foolish enough
to offer conciliation –

the only message a demon understands
is one delivered by blade and blood

must I send an army
to defend your mother's lands

must I remind you of the fate you court
if you fail me again?

aftermath

everywhere I walk
the reek of seaweed rot

* * *

Tom tried his best
to shield me –

the sea demons only
gave their answers
if I was present

they looked at me

saw you

spewed venom

* * *

sea demons flinch from light

I followed the sun

called for candles

glittered with every breath

* * *

I couldn't stay away –

if I closed my eyes
                                        focussed
not on the slither
of obscenities

but on the force and fury

the roiling hate

it could almost have been you
standing in front of me

speaking

the way you spoke to me
the night of the ball

the day I learnt to walk

they say I ran to you –

three toes lost
when they cut off your boot

do you still feel the ache
of kicking me away?

birthright

I must move to the palace

the island is too vulnerable

if I am to rule

I must be seen

to be accepted by the people

have my own guard

reach agreement with my father

Tom's not wrong I know he's not wrong but

his Ma
          and the old baron's widow
                                        are right too –

acting the strumpet
under cover of exile
is one thing

but a maiden trying
to lay claim to her lands
has to be *virgin as snow*

I'll take my place
at the palace
if I have to

but

I can't give him up

yet

a jar of salt crystals

dear father

please find enclosed ~~the crux of the matter~~
all that remains of the writhe of sea demons
that stormed the unscalable cliffs last blood moon

so intent on delivering their message
they tore past the village and hamlets
to rip a path through the forest

~~the waters of the lake churned black~~
~~as they howled their way~~ to the island

~~they came across me~~
I met them at the shoreline
~~they tussled over me dogs with a bone~~

~~Tom my~~
~~my most~~
the head of ~~my stables~~ my personal guard
~~helped me keep them at bay~~ fought by my side
until the rest of his men joined the fray

father – you were ~~as~~ right as always

sea demons can be ~~held off~~ killed
with ~~pitchfork and axe~~ a blade
but it was my cold-cursed touch
that shattered them to salt dust

p.s.

I should ~~perhaps~~ clarify –
the more cherished a sea demon's treasure
the deeper it's buried –

the pack didn't lose three
of their number scaling the cliffs
because these lands offer easy pickings –

your sailors are ~~wantonly~~ wilfully pillaging
the heart and guts of the ocean
the sea demons meant to do the same to you
by despoiling the hidden jewel you hold most dear –

send your army ~~to shore up your defences~~ if you must

but I can promise you this, father –
as long as this is my kingdom
~~however short that reign may be~~
any creature ~~including your proxy~~
~~any of your men~~ that dares defile
the womenfolk under my protection
will be brought before me
and made to kiss my hand

VI

a bold proposal

radiance (dimmed)

take away that girl's glitter
she's probably not even beautiful

if her hair was stripped
of its crystal shimmer

so it lost all trace
of frost-struck heather
on slate mountain side

her eyes would still
                    reflect
the lake serene
on a wintry day

his teeth
        tongue
            fingers
would still
          be eager

                        the shape of her lips
                              the tilt of her chin
            the tiny mole to the left
                        of the dip of her throat –

          to graze
where
        once
            only his gaze could linger

without her glimmer
she'd still unveil slow

skin shivering
at his touch

her laughter pinpricking
him with pleasure

her torrent
          of words
                    cascading
        over him
waking
        shaking him up

till he crawls spent
        gasping to shore

it's not her frost-
                    sparkle
that has him hoarding
the notes she sends

their restrained curves
at odds with their contents –

I want to put my mouth on you

promise made good-*I must be right*
                    you can't even answer me
                    can you, Tom?

                                        give it a rest, Ma

a list of suitors

accursed daughter

yet again you over-reach your authority –

your mother's lands remain in my trust
until the day you wed

when they – and you – become
a husband's concern

consider this latest list of suitors
witless enough to offer for your hand

choose wisely or I shall choose for you –
and this time I shall accept no refusal

each letter from you

I scour for a trace

of the father I make
in these pages

where the more
I open myself

the more
I make of you

yet if I dared write

without thought
without care

the blood and thunder you
would crush me

without thought
without care

first time I saw you

knew I'd kill
to keep you

marry me

not for a kingdom
or to get free
of your father

but because

this life
        frost-life
                no life

you're mine

star-light and ice

low-born demon-born
you won't find better

marry me

hold you fast
long as I can

can't promise
I won't go north

but I'll return
always

marry me

only alive
when I'm with you

won't stop
till you say

don't cry
say yes love

I'm yours

marry me

we fall under your protection

dear father

as you ~~never cease to remind me~~ so rightly state
these are my mother's lands ~~– her people~~

as long as I remain ~~husband- free~~ without husband
we fall under your protection –
and who but a sea demon would risk stirring
the wrath of the conqueror of the cornered lands?

I understand your desire ~~to be rid of me~~ to see me safely wed
~~I too yearn for independence~~
but none of the men on the lists you ~~keep~~ send~~ing~~ will do –

where are the princes of royal blood
with sufficient wealth or military heft
to help me safeguard this realm
~~without your support~~?

~~has it truly escaped your notice~~
it concerns me that all but one ~~(the five-wived sultan)~~
of my latest suitors are from the border lands –
the same ~~ig~~noble houses that covetously skirmish
both our kingdoms –

if I were to marry any one of them –
become wife and widow before the ink
on the deed can freeze –

how soon before my bridegroom's father
or pack of brothers rode to offer aid
or certain retribution

~~*you would still be scrambling your army*~~
how soon before they subjugated these lands
turned their replenished forces toward the storm?

if I have to marry ~~*to secure protection*~~ *–*
and after this latest sea demon assault
I accept I must –

I would respectfully ask not to be ~~*bartered*~~
~~*bound*~~ *allied to a low-born nobleman*

whose death would leave these lands vulnerable
~~*and make us both a laughing stock*~~

instead, father, I would ~~*humbly beg to*~~
marry a man of different blood –

a demon warrior whose reputation burns
beyond the dancing lights of the north
and the blistering isles to the south

whose skill at horse breeding and trading
has lustred the coffers of both our kingdoms

and eased long-held feuds with the mountain clans
and the nomads of the shifting sands

a man who has no interest in kingdom building
save to defend ~~*me*~~ *this land of women to his last bloodied breath*

father, I would seek permission to marry ~~a man~~
the only man I know ~~will give me a wedding night~~
~~can survive~~ unaffected by ~~the hunger~~ ~~the desolation of~~ my touch

the state of you, Tom

can't that girl keep her hands off you
for one night?

startled
into laughter –

pleasure rare

VOWS
VII

a son's love

I'd never kill you, Ma

but call her THAT GIRL
one more time

I'll take my blade
to your tongue

the crippled king's consent

marry your stable-boy if you must –

no man of royal blood would ever soil himself
with a creature such as you –

but if his seed takes twisted root
you shall wake one morning to a sky struck red
the village splintered to kindling
your lands ablaze

you will be dragged from the lake
forced to kneel in ash and gore

made to watch your stable-boy
slaughtered in his stall

if you beg clemency
for the abomination in your womb
accursed daughter you shall receive it –

the swift true mercy of a long-sword's kiss

do you ever wonder

which of us
is the more

disappointed
in the other?

Tom, master of the western marshes

rank water-logged lands
eager to swallow
the unwary

but only a fool
would quibble

at the income
such marshes
will provide

he'll be able
to set up his Ma
in her own cottage

his three older brothers
in their own smallholdings

even buy the stables
and purebreds
from the mistress

if she allows

one last kindness

dear father

please accept my ~~heartfelt~~ sincere gratitude
for granting permission for our marriage

also for your magnanimous ~~gesture~~ gift to my intended
who now has a title and lands to go with his name

I, who have always held titles, the promise of land
would beg one last ~~kindness~~ indulgence, father

please tell me my name

a father's concern

daughter

for the last time –

the naming of a female
is never a father's concern

your names
for there would have been many

can be found
warming your mother in her grave

an exchange of vows

with this silken thread
I bind myself to you

with this leather cord
I bind you to me

with frosted silver
our lives entwine –

three strands made fast
so we are bound

* * *

with this leather cord
I bind myself to you

with frosted silver
I bind you to me

with this silken thread
our lives entwine –

three strands made fast
so we are bound

wedding dress

nine hand-frozen butterflies
for the years we waited

felt longer

six feathers of ice
for the years between us

take my breath
every time

one thousand and one
pressed snowflakes –
the kisses I saved for you

that all?

tiara and slippers of ice
which shattered

like last time

when I kicked them off

come here, wife

under the cherry trees
in the moonlight

dance with me

epilogue

what I know

I don't know if she felt trapped
if she dreamt of running back to her scrublands
I don't know what she'd make of what I've made of her lands
my ice yielding to the sun weeping into the earth
I don't know why she thought a cold spell was the answer
I don't know why she chose my father over the man who loved her
if she even had a choice
I don't know if she'd understand
what she'd make of Tom
what she'd make of me –

her frost-flowers were the making of me